SOUL
Food

· · · · · · ·

RECIPES FOR THE
APPETITE AND SOUL

MCKENZIE E. CARTER

WESTBOW°
PRESS
A DIVISION OF THOMAS NELSON
& ZONDERVAN

WestBow Press books may be ordered through booksellers or by contacting:

WestBow Press
A Division of Thomas Nelson & Zondervan
1663 Liberty Drive
Bloomington, IN 47403
www.westbowpress.com
1 (866) 928-1240

Because of the dynamic nature of the Internet, any web addresses or
links contained in this book may have changed since publication and
may no longer be valid. The views expressed in this work are solely those
of the author and do not necessarily reflect the views of the publisher,
and the publisher hereby disclaims any responsibility for them.

Any people depicted in stock imagery provided by Thinkstock are models,
and such images are being used for illustrative purposes only.
Certain stock imagery © Thinkstock.

ISBN: 978-1-4908-6535-5 (sc)
ISBN: 978-1-4908-6534-8 (e)

Library of Congress Control Number: 2015900359

Print information is available on the last page.

WestBow Press rev. date: 3/4/2015

ACKNOWLEDGEMENTS

I would like to thank several precious people who not only helped make this book possible, but also helped me get the insight for "Recipes for the Soul." First, my wife Cynthia Carter, my mother Laura Almore, my father Alton Henderson, my nephew Kenneth Atkins Jr., my sister Stephanie Carter all of whom have allowed me to inspire them over the years, but unknowingly inspired me with their words and love.

I would like to thank my spiritual father, Dr. Richard Heard, who inspired me to pursue writing this book along with all the precious saints I will mention in the book, and all the individuals who shared recipes with me.

I thank God for the precious congregation of Temple of Deliverance Church in Stafford, Texas that God has blessed me to lead.

Last but not least, I have to give special thanks to my precious wife Cynthia again and my cousin Alisia Robbins who spent much time typing, editing, and giving input to help complete this assignment. I love you greatly and appreciate you. Cynthia you have been a help meet in this book, ministry, and life.

CONTENTS

PREFACE

Growing up as a child in a single parent home I had to learn to cook at an early age. My mother worked long nights to provide for me and my sister. I was a skinny youngster, but had an appetite of a grown man.

My mother and sister labeled me as, "the human garbage disposal" because I would destroy any food in sight. I still remember my mother's reaction while watching me eat. She had a disturbed look on her face while shaking her head saying, "Boy, you must have a tape worm!"

By having the appetite of a grown man and my mother working nights my sister and I had to learn to cook fast. This meant us having to get as much skill in the art of cooking as soon as possible. My hunger compelled me to start asking people how to cook different meals. Even as I got a little older I would never hesitate to call my love ones, "mostly from the country," to ask them how to cook certain foods. One thing I learned quickly was if I used the same ingredients they used and followed the exact steps they gave me I would end with a dish that had the same great taste as their food.

If you have the right source, the right ingredients, the right directions, and a willingness to follow the instructions given then delicious food should be the end result. I have found out that life can many times operate under the same principle. The right source, the right ingredients, the right directions given in life, and a willingness to follow instructions given can cause us to have a life that can be favored by the presence of God. Like a delicious meal prepared and placed on the table people will be drawn to our lives, pull up a chair, sit down at the table, say grace, and begin to feast on the glorious delectable spiritual meal, that comes from a life that has gone through the same process God used in Matthew 14 when he fed over 5,000 people with 5 loaves and 2 fish. God blesses us, he allows us to go thru events that lead us to be broken before him, and then he gives us away to meet the needs of people that need to be fed.

This book consists of 11 simple recipes for the appetite that I received mostly from precious people that I love who knows how to make it happen in the kitchen, but it also consists of next to salvation some of the most important spiritual lessons that I have learned in my walk with God. I believe these "Recipes for the Appetite and Soul," will tremendously bless your life.

In the "Recipes for the Appetite and Soul," I tell you the name of the person God used to inspire and teach me life's lesson and in "Soul-Food," I also tell the name of the person that gave me the recipe.

May this book be a blessing to you and your household. Just remember that regardless of which recipe you are looking at rather it is "Recipe for the Appetite and Soul" or "Soul-Food" they both require a few things to be a success. Again the right source, the right ingredients, the right directions, and a willingness to follow the instructions given.

As you continue to read this book please read it with this question in mind. "Are you at a place in your life where you no longer want to waste any more precious time and desire to see kingdom results?" If so, let's flip the recipe for success in the kitchen and in life and see if you are ready to experience the best results by learning how to apply kingdom principles.

1. Are we connected to the right source?"
2. Do we have the right ingredients?
3. Have we received the right instructions?
4. Are we willing to follow the instructions given?

My prayer is that this book will be used as a tool to ignite a hunger in you to get kingdom results!

A Recipe for Wisdom

Scriptural reference: Proverbs 4:7 (King James Version)

*"Wisdom is the principal thing; therefore get wisdom:
and with all thy getting get understanding."*

INGREDIENTS FOUND IN THIS CHAPTER:

1. A definition of wisdom
2. Benefits of receiving the wisdom of God
3. Five ways to receive the wisdom of God

The person God used to impart wisdom in my life and place me on a quest to receive more wisdom was my late great-uncle Charlie. Although God used many people to impart wisdom in my life, I choose to talk about him and dedicate this chapter in honor of him because God used him to impart wisdom to me at a very important time in my life. God used him to help teach me how to be a man of God, a husband, and a spiritual leader.

A RECIPE FOR WISDOM

In order to understand the meaning of wisdom, it is necessary to look at the difference between knowledge and wisdom. Knowledge can be defined as facts and information that one acquires from study or education. Wisdom is the ability to apply the right information in the right situation. Additionally, there are at least two kinds of wisdom that are mentioned in the Bible.

James 3:13-18 (New International Version) says the following:

> *Who is wise and understanding among you? Let them show it by their good life, by deeds done in humility that comes from wisdom. But if you harbor bitter envy and selfish ambition in your hearts, do not boast about it or deny the truth. Such "wisdom" does not come down from heaven but is earthly, unspiritual, demonic. For where you have envy and selfish ambition, there you find disorder and every evil practice. But the wisdom that comes from heaven is first of all pure; then peace-loving, considerate, submissive, full of mercy and good fruit, impartial and sincere. Peacemakers who sow in peace reap a harvest of righteousness.*

For a Christian I believe that godly wisdom can be defined as, the ability to make godly decisions based on the Word of God, godly counsel, the leading of the Holy Spirit, and godly convictions. When I think of the word wisdom immediately I think of Solomon from the Bible. Solomon was the son of David and Bathsheba and became the third king of Israel. Solomon was known for his wisdom. Listen to the conversation between God and Solomon that led to Solomon receiving wisdom.

1 Kings 3:5-14 (NIV) reads as,

> *At Gibeon the Lord appeared to Solomon during the night in a dream, and God said, "Ask for whatever you want me to give you." Solomon answered, "You have shown great kindness to your servant, my father David, because he was faithful to you and righteous and upright in heart. You have continued this great kindness to him and have given him a son to sit on his throne this very day. "Now, Lord my God, you have made your servant king in place of my father David. But I am only a little child and do not know how to carry out my duties. Your servant is here among the people you have chosen, a great people, too numerous to count or number. So give your servant a discerning heart to govern your people and to distinguish between right and wrong. For who is able to govern this great people of yours?" The Lord was pleased that Solomon had asked for this. So God said to him, "Since you asked for this and not for long life or wealth for yourself, nor have asked for the death of your enemies but for discernment in administering justice, I will do what you have asked. I will give you a wise and discerning heart, so that there will never have been anyone like you, nor will there ever be. Moreover, I will give you what you have not asked for ---both wealth and honor---so that in your lifetime you will have no equal among kings. And if you walk in obedience to me and keep my decrees and commands as David your father did, I will give you a long life.*

Wow, imagine God appearing to Solomon in a dream and saying, "Ask for whatever you want me to give you.

Solomon replies, give me a discerning heart to govern your people." He basically asks for wisdom and this pleases God so much. God says he will give Solomon wisdom, riches, and honor. Also if Solomon walks in obedience, he will lengthen his days. Now that's a good deal! Somebody say, "Come here, wisdom!"

There are several principles in this passage that are transformational. Let's talk about the benefits of receiving wisdom.

FIRST BENEFIT OF RECEIVING WISDOM: IT PLEASES GOD WHEN WE ASK FOR WISDOM

1 Kings 3:10 (NIV) says, *"The Lord was pleased that Solomon had asked for this."* God is pleased when we ask him for his wisdom because what we are saying is, *"Tell me how to do it your way."* Those that refuse to obey God and receive the wisdom of God are usually those who, like most of us, spent a significant amount of time trying to do it our way while making one bad decision after another until we realize our way doesn't work.

Proverbs 14:12 (NIV) says, *"There is a way that appears to be right, but in the end it leads to death."* We usually try life our way until we bump our heads a couple of times finally realizing it's time to do it God's way.

Proverbs 9:10 (NIV) says, *"The fear of the Lord is the beginning of wisdom, and knowledge of the Holy One is understanding."* Our pathway to wisdom begins when we accept Christ as Savior and continues as we realize the principles taught in Deuteronomy 28 which are that if we obey God we experience a life of blessings and fulfillment, but if we disobey him we experience the consequences of disobedience and curses.

SECOND BENEFIT OF RECEIVING WISDOM: IT GIVES US THE ABILITY TO MAKE WISE DECISIONS

Right after Solomon asked for wisdom from God, Solomon was faced with a difficult decision. He had to use godly wisdom to make a very difficult decision. 1 Kings 3:16-28 (NIV) says:

Now two prostitutes came to the king and stood before him. One of them said, "Pardon me, my lord. This woman and I live in the same house, and I had a baby while she was there with me. The third day after my child was born, this woman also had a baby. We were alone; there was no one in the house but the two of us.

"During the night this woman's son died because she lay on him. So she got up in the middle of the night and took my son from my side while I your servant was asleep. She put him by her breast and put her dead son by my breast. The next morning, I got up to nurse my son---and he was dead! But when I looked at him closely in the morning light, I saw that it wasn't the son I had borne." The other woman said, "No! The living one is my son; the dead one is yours." But the first one insisted, "No! The dead one is yours; the living one is mine." And so they argued before the king. The king said, "This one says, "My son is alive and your son is dead," while that one says, "No! Your son is dead and mine is alive." Then the king said, "Bring me a sword." So they brought a sword for the king. He then gave an order: "Cut the living child in two and give half to one and half to the other." The woman whose son was alive was deeply moved out of love for her son and said to the king, "Please, my lord,

give her the living baby! Don't kill him!" But the other said, Neither I nor you shall have him. Cut him in two!" Then the king gave his ruling: Give the living baby to the first woman. Do not kill him; she is his mother." When all Israel heard the verdict the king had given, they held the king in awe, because they saw that he had wisdom from God to administer justice.

Now this was a big decision for the newly appointed king to make, but the wisdom that Solomon received from God equipped and empowered him to make the right decision. If Solomon would have made the wrong choice in this situation more than likely the people he was called to lead would have lost confidence in him. While not being exempt from making a bad decision, godly wisdom allows us to walk with God, because of our willingness to seek God and spend time with him. We should be able to make wise decisions and echo the heart of God to his people.

One of the things I have discovered in my years of pastoring is that in order to make decisions in dealing with people we have to know the Word of God, be prayerful, be able to carefully hear the voice of God, listen to the facts being presented, weigh them, use discernment, and then make decisions by filtering the information we have received using a spiritual process.

Sometimes we have to resist the temptation to make decisions on the spot. While some things may need to be addressed on the spot I have found in most cases it is okay to say, "Let me pray about it and get back with you," or simply, "Let me get back to you on that." The temptation is to sometimes out of pride give an answer too quickly. Sometimes we act as if we have all the right answers which can lead to us giving bad advice, wrong advice, or just flat out making bad decisions. When I don't know the answer I sometimes asks the person how soon they need to know. If someone is asking me to do something that I'm not sure about then I pray about it, receive wisdom from God, and then answer them.

Decisions can help determine the direction of your destiny. We can make an unwise decision that will not only affect us, but those around us for years. Most of us are where we are in life presently as a result of decisions we made in our past. "Ouch, Praise God, and Amen!" While none of us can honestly say every decision we made has been the right decision or that we won't make any more unwise decisions we can decide from this point on that we will try our best to receive the wisdom of God in making decisions in our life.

If we do what Proverbs 3:5-6 (KJV) says, *"Trust in the Lord with all your heart; and lean not unto thine own understanding. In all thy ways acknowledge him, and he shall direct thy paths."*

HERE ARE SEVERAL POWERFUL INSTRUCTIONS GIVEN IN THESE FEW VERSES:

1. Trust in the Lord. This takes faith in God.
2. Lean not unto thy own understanding. This takes humility. The Message Bible says, "Don't try to figure out everything on your own."
3. Acknowledge God in all your ways. This takes consistency and commitment.

Now let's look at the awesome promise made, *"In all thy ways acknowledge him, and he shall direct thy paths"* (Prov.3:6). We need to start crying out for the wisdom of God and receive it. As we receive God's wisdom we need to make scriptural declarations like Psalms 37:23 (KJV) that reads, *"The steps of a good man are ordered by the Lord: and he delighteth in his way."*

I believe many times we make bad decisions simply because we fail to slow down and seek God to receive wisdom to make wise decisions. Proverbs 28:5 (KJV) states something powerful. *"Evil men understand not judgment: but they that seek the Lord understand all things."*

Make a decision to seek God's direction like never before especially when making major decisions like, who you will marry, where you will live, and what career path you will take. God wrote the script of your life, directed it, and produced it. God gets joy in directing us on what to do in each scene. Remember he knows the conclusion.

CHAPTER 2

How to Receive the Wisdom of God

I believe there are at least three ways to receive God's wisdom based on what I have learned from the word of God and experienced personally in life.

THE FIRST WAY TO RECEIVE WISDOM: BY ACCEPTING CHRIST AS OUR LORD AND SAVIOR

Proverbs 9:10 (KJV) *"The fear of the Lord is the beginning of wisdom: and the knowledge of the holy is understanding."* 1 Corinthians 1:30 (KJV) *"But of him are ye in Christ Jesus, who of God is made unto us wisdom, and righteousness, and sanctification, and redemption."*

Accepting Christ is the start of our quest for wisdom. We don't accept Christ just to get wisdom, but we receive wisdom as a result of accepting Christ.

Ephesians 1:13-14 (KJV) *"In whom ye also trusted, after that ye heard the word of truth, the gospel of your salvation: in whom also after that ye believed, ye were sealed with that holy Spirit of promise, Which is the earnest of our inheritance until the redemption of the purchased possession, unto the praise of his glory."*

Once an individual receives Christ as their Savior they receive the Holy Spirit. I believe that a believer should earnestly desire more of God. Matthew 5:6 (KJV) says, *"Blessed are they which do hunger and thirst after righteousness: for they shall be filled."* As we hunger and seek more of God, he will fill us with his Spirit in a way that will transform our lives.

By receiving Christ and by God's spirit living in us we automatically begin to tap into the wisdom of God that's in us because of the Holy Spirit. In the book of Isaiah the Holy Spirit is referred to as the spirit of wisdom. As we yield ourselves to God's face in prayer we begin to walk in the wisdom of God. If you have accepted Christ ponder on this thought for a moment:

Although we can and do make unwise decisions, after we are saved, imagine how many bad decisions you would have made in between the time you accepted Christ and now if you weren't saved. Accepting Christ literally causes you to live and think in another dimension especially once the process of renewing your mind begins. You begin to experience kingdom thinking. The closer you get to God you will find yourself making more and more wise decisions.

Sometimes I look back at my past and some of the things I have done I shake my head at my own self, but the episode usually ends with me thanking God for my deliverance.

Before I move to the next way to receive the wisdom of God, I want to take the time to speak to someone who may be reading this book who may not have accepted Christ. There may also be someone who have experienced church, but have not really experienced Christ. If you are reading this book and are not sure of your salvation, accepting Christ will be the wisest decision you can ever make in your life.

Based upon Romans 10:9 (KJV) say this prayer with me:

Lord Jesus, I repent of every sin that I have committed and I ask you to forgive me for all my sins. I believe that you died for my sins and I believe that you were raised from the dead, so that I might experience eternal life. Come into my heart, save me, fill me with your Spirit, and help me to live a life that will glorify you in Jesus name.

If you prayed this prayer, believed it, and meant it, welcome to the family of God. Now that you are saved if you haven't already connected to a Spirit filled bible teaching church, ask the Lord to lead you to one, so you can get connected to a church family vision, and godly leadership that will pray for you and begin to disciple you.

THE SECOND WAY TO RECEIVE WISDOM: THROUGH THE READING, MEDITATING, AND STUDYING OF THE WORD OF GOD

The Word of God is the will of God. Once we're saved and begin to read, study, and meditate on the Word of God we begin the process of renewing our mind. The Word of God has power to literally help fashion the way we think and if we change the way we think we can change the way we live.

The first part of Proverbs 23:7 (KJV) says, "For as he thinketh in his heart, so is he…" Reading and applying the Word of God makes us wiser. Psalms 119 (KJV) which happens to be the passage with the most verses in the Bible talks a lot about the Word.

> "O how love I thy law! It is my meditation all the day (v. 97). I have more understanding than all my teachers: for thy testimonies are my meditation (v. 99). I understand more than the ancients, because I keep thy precepts (v. 100)."

II. Timothy 3:15 (KJV) *"And that from a child thou hast known the holy scriptures, which are able to make thee wise unto salvation through faith which is in Christ Jesus."*

By learning the Word of God, God begins to teach us how to live for him, make decisions, and live a life that will cause us to walk in perpetual blessings and peace. On the other hand, the life of someone who is unsaved and not submitted to the Word of God usually live their life making one bad decision after another and spend a lot of time regretting the consequences of the unwise decisions they made.

THE THIRD WAY TO RECEIVE WISDOM: PRAYER

It almost sounds too good to be true, but the truth is you may just be one prayer away from the wisdom you need. James 1:5 (KJV) is a verse I have begun to live by. It reads, *"If any of you lack wisdom, let him ask of God, that giveth to all men liberally, and upbraideth not; and it shall be given him."* What a remarkable promise. God says if you need wisdom simply ask me for it. I have asked God for wisdom, so much in the past twelve years of my life that it has become a regular part of my prayer life. I recently thought about the fact that it takes humility to pray because you are praying for God's will to be done in your life and not your own (Matthew 26:39 KJV). We are literally telling God I don't know what to do unless you speak to me if not I will probably make the wrong decisions. I believe God loves when we pray because it's expressing to our heavenly Father that we need him and we want to do things his way.

Just imagine how much heartache could have been prevented if we would have asked God to give us wisdom before we got involved in some of the relationships we got involved in. Imagine how much money we could have sowed, saved, and spent with purpose attached to it instead of wasting it. We could have started years ago asking God for wisdom on how to use our finances wisely. I have found out the wisdom of God helps us to make the right decisions instead of using the process of elimination, which causes us to work thru all the incorrect answers before we arrive at the right one. That may be helpful when taking a test, but it can sometimes be time consuming when it comes to life. While realizing that we are imperfect beings, no matter how anointed we are, praying for wisdom may not cause us to live a perfect life, but it will definitely help us make more wise decisions and have less regrets.

After Solomon prayed for wisdom, God said in 1 Kings 3:12 (KJV), *"Behold, I have done according to thy words: lo, I have given thee a wise and an understanding heart; so that there was none like thee before thee, neither after thee shall any arise like unto thee."* The wisdom of God will cause you to excel in every area of your life. Praying for God's wisdom in other words says; show me your choice, the right way.

I advise every child of God that's reading this book to start praying regularly for God's wisdom on a regular basis. I learned this simple, but powerful principle when I began serving as interim pastor of a church. After only being in ministry for two years, God's anointing was on me, but there was a huge responsibility before me which was more than just preaching a sermon, hugging a few people, and going home. I realized I now had to preach and lead God's people in the things of God. I prayed for wisdom on what to minister on Sundays, what to say in meetings, what to say in counseling sessions, and how to handle different personalities. I watched God from that point in my life to this point consistently give me the wisdom I needed to lead his people. Since we know that the steps of a good man are ordered by the Lord it would be wise to stay in constant communion with God while and before taking steps.

You may or may not be the pastor of a church, so you may not need God's wisdom to pastor a church, however you do need God's wisdom to be the church and manifest the kingdom of God. You also need God's wisdom to show the world that Christians are a blessed people who have been placed here by God to manifest the glory of God in every area of our life.

Be encouraged you're being led by God even as you're reading this book. Make declarations that you are wiser than you were last year and you will walk in the wisdom of God until your time is up here on earth. It's not that we won't ever miss God, but what I love about God is when you're his child and you're praying if your heart is right towards him even when you miss him his hands are big enough to catch you.

Praise God your assignment is to start praying on a regular basis for the wisdom of God and believe he's going to give it to you. In James 1:6-7 (KJV), God's wisdom is waiting for us to tap into his abundant provision. James 4:2 (KJV) Part B reads, *"...Yet ye have not, because ye ask not."* Let's start asking for, receiving, and walking in the wisdom of God.

THE FOURTH WAY TO RECEIVE WISDOM IS THRU THE ADVICE AND COUNSEL OF GODLY MEN AND WOMEN OF GOD

"He that walketh with wise men shall be wise: but a companion of fools shall be destroyed" Proverbs 13:20 (KJV).Words are so powerful that we can read in Genesis 1 as God created the world he began to speak things into existence. One would think that something as marvelous as the creation of the

world would have required more effort. Genesis 1:3 reads, *"And God said, Let there be light: and there was light."* Second day God said, *"Let there be a firmament in the midst of the waters and let it divide the waters from the waters"* (v.6). God continued speaking things into existence. The Bible says, *"Death and life are in the power of the tongue: and they that love it shall eat the fruit thereof"* Proverbs 18:21 (KJV). The latter part of Romans 4:17 (KJV) reads, *"…God, who quickeneth the dead, and calleth those things which be not as though they were."* Over and over in the Word of God we see the power of words.

In what we call the Great Commission in Matthew 28:19,20 reads, *"Go ye therefore, and teach all nations, baptizing them in the name of the Father, and of the Son, and of the Holy Ghost: Teaching them to observe all things whatsoever I have commanded you: and, lo, I am with you alway, even unto the end of the world. Amen."* The word teaching in (v. 20) has a powerful meaning. The Greek word for teaching here is didasko which means to know, to teach, instruct by word of mouth, and it is also the shaping of the will of the pupil which also helps me to understand discipleship and becoming Christ-like.

As I abide in Christ, spend time with God, receive his Word, and his teachings he begins to shape my will. Words are so powerful that they can shape and influence the will of the listener, so as it relates to wisdom if I hearken to words of someone with godly wisdom I will become wise. If I hang around someone who constantly talks foolishly if I'm not careful their foolish talk can begin to affect my thinking and begin to shape my will. One that wants to become wise should walk with wise men. Now I understand why I always had a love for older people. My mother once told me I was like an old man trapped in a young man's body. Now it's plain to me that God had placed a desire in me to attain wisdom. I believe a lot of children love their grandparents because they love spending time with them especially during the summer. One reason I loved spending time with my grandmothers because both of them liked to cook, and I like to eat. Another reason is because my grandmothers on both sides had a way of making me feel like I was their favorite grandchild by their actions and words. As I matured my reasons for wanting to be around them and other older people changed. I then realized I desired their wisdom. I now view older saints that have walked with God faithfully as walking treasure chests. When I sense I'm talking to a godly seasoned saint I position myself as a student sitting on the edge of my chair as I listen to my favorite lecturer not wanting to miss a word.

My inspiration for writing on wisdom is my great uncle Charlie. When Uncle Charlie passed away he was about 94 years old. I remember seeing Uncle Charlie over the years at family reunions, and back then my thought in seeing him was, "man that must be my oldest relative." What I didn't realize was that he was a walking treasure chest.

Around 1996 or 1997 I began to sense it was something God wanted me to do. I had a feeling it was to preach, however I wasn't fully convinced. I was running from the responsibility of that which I wasn't even fully convinced of. My thought was, "I'm young and the party is just starting. I can't party and be a minister." Finally, the calling was so strong on my heart I knew I needed to talk to someone about it.

I was led to talk to a very humble, but powerful and influential pastor in Beaumont, Texas Pastor Delbert Mack of the Cathedral of Faith Church. He was the assistant pastor for years to Dr. T.R. Williams of the New Faith Church in Houston, Texas which is the same church I grew up in. Although I didn't know Pastor Mack personally he was a vessel that God used to preach a message that led me to accepting Christ. Now I sense the Holy Spirit leading me to go to Beaumont, Texas and meet with Pastor Mack and discuss the feelings I had been experiencing. I called Pastor Mack and he agreed to meet with me. My only concern now was how I would find his church.

The Lord set it up, so that I ran into my Uncle Charlie at our yearly family reunion in 1999. I told him I wanted to come to Beaumont to find Pastor Mack's church and he said, "You can come spend the night with me and I will show you how to get to get to his church." Little did I know I had a date with destiny. I was about to begin wisdom 101.

The next day I made it to my Uncle Charlie's house and one thing that let me know we were kin is that we both love to eat. We ate and talked almost all night at the kitchen table. I poured out my heart and feelings to him. After Uncle Charlie listened to me a little while he said, "you're like Saul going down Damascus Road in Acts 9." He told me I was called to preach. My next question was, "Can I wait a little while before I do?" I thought to myself, "I wanted to go to one more spring break Kappa Beach Party in Galveston, Texas and one more after party in New Orleans on Bourbon Street following the Bayou Classic football game." Uncle Charlie looked at me and said, "If you put God on hold you're going to miss his blessings." Although I was still carnal at the time I didn't want to miss any blessings, so I was prepared to say, "Yes."

Uncle Charlie and I really connected as we talked the entire night. Now all of a sudden the precious man I thought of as my oldest uncle with grey hair is being established in my life as a priceless mentor. The next day Uncle Charlie led me to Pastor Mack's church. As I went in his office and sat down to talk I told him who I was and the strong feelings I was having. He looked at me and said, "You are called to preach, you are like Saul going down Damascus Road in Acts 9." I tried the same question on him about buying time as I asked Uncle Charlie. I asked, "What do I do now that I know, do I wait a little while?" He said, "No, now that you know what God wants you to do you just need to obey him." He advised me to meet with my Pastor and talk to him.

So I drove to Houston and met with my Pastor at that time it was Dr. T.R. Williams. It was about a year from the time I met with my Pastor and I preached my first sermon. During this year I committed myself to the things of God and begin to spend regular time with God. I preached my first sermon on March 22, 2000 and have still been as hungry for godly wisdom as when I first started ministering. I had a million questions to ask my Uncle Charlie about ministry and life itself. It's important for you to know that at this time I was still dating my wife Cynthia. We married on November 9, 2002, so God allowed me to connect with Uncle Charlie for a least two major transitions in my life, marriage and ministry. From the day we had that talk in his kitchen we connected on a level that is unexplainable. As my mentor he became the teacher and I became the student. I found out a valuable lesson while receiving counsel from him. The amount of wisdom a mentor can release in the mentee's life is determined by the level of hunger the mentee has for wisdom and the amount of honor they have for their mentor. Transformation cannot take place when the one who has the authority and revelation to release wisdom and bring change is not honored. We saw this principle during the ministry of Jesus.

In Mark 6:1-6 (KJV) reads, *"And he went out from thence, and came into his own country; and his disciples follow him.*

And when the sabbath day was come, he began to teach in the synagogue: and many hearing him were astonished, saying, From whence hath this man these things? and what wisdom is this which is given unto him, that even such mighty works are wrought by his hands? Is not this the carpenter, the son of Mary, the brother of James, and Joses, and of Judas, and Simon? and are not his sisters here with us? And they were offended at him. But Jesus, said unto them, A prophet is not without honour, but in his own country, and among his own kin, and in his own house. And he could there do no mighty work, save that he laid his hands upon a few sick folk, and healed them. And he marveled because of their unbelief. And he went round about the villages, teaching."

This passage was mainly about the people's unbelief however, there are several powerful principles in these verses that can impact our lives profoundly concerning receiving wisdom thru advice and the counsel of godly men and women of God.

Familiarity without wisdom can cause you to reject anointed men and women of God that God has placed in your life to minister to you. When there is dishonor and unbelief God's revelation and power can be hindered. When the student shows up ready to receive, their hunger for wisdom unlocks the divine storage of precious jewels inside the teacher that can allow the godly man or woman of God to say things that will literally transform that person's life forever.

The same way the bible says in Acts 22:3 (KJV), Paul was brought up in the city at the feet of Gamaliel and taught according to the perfect manner of the law of the fathers. I sat at the feet of my uncle and received wisdom that has impacted me in a way I will never forget.

Every Sunday evening he made time to talk to me. I would call him with questions about life, marriage, ministry, and he would spend sometimes an hour or two pouring into me the wisdom of God. I have a black binder with dividers in it and one section labeled, "Uncle Charlie Speaks." I wrote down the things he said because I knew they were inspired by God. When I had a problem I would simply call him and say: Great Uncle, I need some power steering and as soon as he opened his mouth the wisdom of God started flowing and I soaked it up like a sponge. Some years back he got ill, but even before he got sick I spent time with him. I would go to see him and whatever he wanted me to do I would do it as it pertained to honoring and serving him. I remember having the honor of even feeding him before he went into the hospital and passed away. I cried when he passed, but I thanked God for the things that he spoke over me and that has helped mold me into who I am today.

Never underestimate the priceless value of God placing people in your life to speak words of wisdom.

THE FIFTH WAY TO RECEIVE WISDOM: THRU LIFE EXPERIENCES

Proverbs 5:1 (Amplified Version) *"MY SON, be attentive to my Wisdom [godly Wisdom learned by actual and costly experience], and incline your ear to my understanding [of what is becoming and prudent for you]."* We have learned that wisdom can be received thru accepting Christ as Savior through reading, studying, and meditating in the Word of God, prayer thru the advice and counsel of godly men and women of God, and now thru life experiences.

Notice that this verse says that this wisdom is learned by actual and costly experience. While the other ways of receiving wisdom didn't seem difficult to attain, this way of receiving wisdom comes by actual and costly experience.

There are some lessons in life that are costly. The amazing thing about being a child of God is that even when we mess up big time God can take our past mistakes and use them as lifelong reminders that some roads we take in life can lead to pain, but there are some lessons we learn by walking thru some things, "Life 101." There are certain tests we must take in life, but God loves us so much if we fail the test we can take it again. If you're like me there are some experiences that if I have a vote, I wouldn't want to go thru again.

When a child of God walks with God even in our storms we can ask God in prayer, "What is the lesson I can learn from this?" I have decided and accepted there are inevitable challenges we have to face in life and it would be wise to decide to not go thru difficult places in life and come out empty handed. Some of you may say how can something good come out of this, but God can give us wisdom for our future. A testimony of his faithfulness and revelation that sometimes the only way out is thru. It may take some time before we realize how some experiences made us stronger and wiser, but we will.

I want to stop and encourage somebody going thru a fire. It is wisdom on the other side of this fiery furnace. It is wisdom on the other side of this storm, and it is somebody waiting to be ministered to thru the testimony and wisdom you have attained. In Mark 5:1, Jesus had just spoke peace in the middle of the storm and once He and the disciples reached the other side of the sea there was a man in need of deliverance waiting to be ministered to by Jesus. When you come out this storm you're going to come out with wisdom and a testimony that will break some other person's chains. The bad relationship prepared you for your God ordained relationship. Sometimes you won't understand order until you have lived in confusion. The pain that comes along with making bad decisions can get you to a point where you pray before making every decision.

It's only after we have attained wisdom thru actual and costly experience that we really understand. *"And we know that all things work together for good to them that love God, to them who are the called according to his purpose"* Romans 8:28 (KJV).Then we can talk like David talked in Psalms 119:71 (KJV*), "It is good for me that I have been afflicted; that I might learn thy statutes."* Praise God!

BONUS PAGE
WISE SAYINGS

In my quest for wisdom, one of the things that I have learned is that all of my mentors and godly influences in my life all have wise sayings that was passed on to them from someone else. These sayings are timeless and loaded with meaning, so I took the time to list some and I pray they will be a blessing to you.

As you enjoy these wise sayings I encourage you to also reflect on the wise sayings of your parents, mentors, teachers, leaders, or other love ones that will forever be a part of who you are today. Thank God for that person's influence in your life.

1ST WISE SAYING:

- Don't put the cart before the horse.

Meaning--Don't do things in the wrong order by being impatient.

I learned this wise saying from my late Great Uncle Charlie Henderson who has transitioned into the presence of God.

2ND WISE SAYING:

- Every tub must stand on its own bottom.

Meaning--People should be responsible and independent when necessary.

I learned this wise saying from my mother, Laura Almore, who learned it from her mother, Maugerite Freeman, my grandmother.

3RD WISE SAYING:

- You can lead a horse to water, but you can't make it drink.

Meaning--You can present someone with an opportunity, but you cannot force him or her to take advantage of it.

I learned this wise saying from my mother, Laura Almore, who learned it from her mother, Maugerite Freeman, my grandmother.

4TH WISE SAYING:

- Don't take any wooden nickels.

Meaning-- Be alert and exercise caution in what you are doing. Don't allow people to get over on you.

I learned this wise saying from my Aunt Connie Paintsil, who learned it from her mother, which is my grandmother, Maugerite Henderson.

5TH WISE SAYING:

- All that glitters is not gold.

Meaning--The attractive external appearance of something is not a reliable indication of its true nature.

I learned this wise saying from my Aunt Connie Paintsill, who learned it from her mother, which is my grandmother, Maugerite Henderson.

6TH WISE SAYING:

- Feed them with a long handled spoon.

Meaning--There is certain people in life that you have to keep at a distance.

I learned this wise saying from my mother, Laura Almore, who learned it from her mother, my grandmother, Maugerite Freeman.

7TH WISE SAYING:

- A bird in the hand is better than two in the bush.

Meaning--It is better to have something that is certain than a risk to get more, where you might lose everything.

I learned this wise saying from my mentor, Dr. Guthrie, who learned it from her father, Pastor Manuel Washington.

CHAPTER 3
A RECIPE FOR LOVE

Scriptural reference: Ephesians 5:1-2 (KJV) *"Be ye therefore followers of God, as dear children; And walk in love, as Christ also hath loved us, and hath given himself for us an offering and a sacrifice to God for a sweet-smelling savour."*

INGREDIENTS FOUND IN THIS CHAPTER:
1. Love shown by sacrifice
2. Walking in love

INDIVIDUALS THAT GOD USED TO DEMONSTRATE THE LOVE OF GOD:
1. My Mother Laura Almore
2. My Aunt Rosemary Robbins

We know that love is powerful because John 3:16 (KJV) says *"For God so loved the world, that he gave his only begotten Son, that whosoever believeth in him should not perish, but have everlasting life."* And 1 John 4:8 (KJV) reads, *"He that loveth not knoweth not God; for God is love."* We should never question God's love for us when we understand that God sent Jesus to die for our sins. If we accept him we could have eternal life. There are so many people that God has used to show me the love of God, but I chose to talk about the first two individuals that came to my mind.

My mother is one of the sweetest individuals I have ever known. She is so precious that you have this feeling of acceptance when you're in her presence. Here love is visible and tangible. She is the type that when she walks in the room it seems like the atmosphere lights up. I treasure her dearly and thank God for blessing me with a mother that has loved me unconditionally all of my life.

My Aunt Rose was another precious gift placed in my life that walked in the love of God. She wasn't selective with who she demonstrated love to, and she made everyone she met feel loved. She has transitioned into the presence of the Lord and although she is not here physically the impact she made lives on. I am also grateful for my cousins her twin daughters Alisha and Alisia who both have been a tremendous blessing to me in many ways. I see parts of her character in both of them. Much love to her son Mc Ray Robbins Jr. who passed away a couple of years ago.

Love God, yourself, your family, people, your enemies, and life because it's a gift from God. Choose love over hatred and walk in the love of God.

LOVE SHOWN BY SACRIFICE

The definition of sacrifice is destruction or surrender of something for the sake of something else; something given up or something lost.

We know that the greatest sacrifice that was ever made was at Calvary as Jesus died for our redemption. I now would like to tell you about a type of sacrifice that takes place every day in this world that needs to be acknowledged. That is the sacrifice that loving parents make for their children and the giving of themselves on a daily basis.

My mother is one of the hardest working individuals

I have ever known. Her love for my sister and I have been demonstrated over the years in many ways. In the way she treated us, provided for us, and how she raised us to believe in and serve God, as well as her continued support in our lives now. My mother as a single parent would sometimes work twelve hour shifts to provide for us. I remember her going to work at 4:00am and not getting off until 12:00 pm the next day. She never complained about having to provide for us or about being tired. She just did what she had to do to provide and take care of us. One of the things I still find amazing is how she sacrificed and worked, so hard but yet also made sure she spent time with us and took us to church every Sunday. It was through her pressing her way to get to church that I learned the principles of giving tithes and offerings at a young age by seeing her consistently paying her tithes over the years. I still remember on one occasion sitting next to her in church being upset because I didn't understand why she was putting that much money in the offering basket. I looked as she placed the money in the basket and said, "Momma, I need some new shoes." I didn't realize that even then God was using her commitment to Him to model in me what it means to remain committed to God in spite of what season you are in life.

Remember that the word sacrifice means something given up. When parents sacrifice (go without) for their children to have that's a powerful demonstration of how the love of a parent will motivate them to work hard and go without, so their children can have everything they need.

As a young child I loved to crack jokes and make people laugh. When I was in school we called it ranking on someone. On one particular day I tried to crack a joke on my mother and was humbled by the feedback I got. My mother has always been a beautiful lady who kept a neat and clean appearance, but on this occasion I remember trying to be funny by asking her, "Momma, why you have on those old beat up jeans?" She responded, "So I can afford to buy you some new ones." I was humbled when I realized she went without new clothes, so we could have new clothes.

Another way I realized loving parents demonstrate their love for their children thru sacrifice is by putting their dreams on hold. My mother worked for thirty years at the post office to earn a living for our family. It's amazing when you're a child being supported by your parent you usually don't take into consideration they have dreams, goals, and aspirations as well. It took me a while to realize my mother had things she desired to do that were on hold because she was so busy working, keeping us in church, and trying to raise us. She sacrificed her own goals to make sure we were well taken care of. My mother was 40 years old when she decided to go to college and pursue her dreams. She worked hard while continuing to work at the post office. She went to school and stayed active in ministry. I was so proud of her when she graduated, retired from the post office, and now fulfilling one of her dreams by serving as a licensed Family Therapist helping countless families that come to her for counsel. While doing that she is also an ordained minister of the Gospel of Jesus Christ serving faithfully at the church I Pastor. It is an honor for me to have her serving with me in ministry. It's amazing how God works. She sacrificed her dreams for a season and God blessed her with a son that has been called to be a leader in the body of Christ. We have a unique relationship in that I'm her son, but also her Pastor and spiritual father. She was also blessed in the sense that my sister has gone to college, graduated, and working in the field she desired to work in.

I say this to encourage some parent, grandparent, or

love one who are raising children just know that your hard work and sacrifice will pay off as long as you continue to put God first. You could be raising a leader, a president, a teacher, or someone who God is going to use to impact this nation. Trust God to bless your sacrifice made and praise him for the future kings and queens that you are raising or have already raised.

I have watched my mother make many sacrifices to help others and demonstrate the love of God at times to people who may or may not have appreciated her as she went through things and at times went thru seasons of brokenness. But remember many times your brokenness will lead to someone else's feast. When Jesus fed the multitude in Matthew 14:19 (KJV) says, *"…took the five loaves, and the two fishes, and looking up to heaven, he blessed, and brake, and gave the loaves to his disciples, and the disciples to the multitudes."* What am I saying? When you love God and love people there will be times when you have to make sacrifices in life and at times there will be seasons of trials and you may experience a brokenness, but remember God is going to use your brokenness to minister his love to others. Once we're in his hands he blesses us initially at salvation. The richest blessing is accepting his redemption. He allows us to experience brokenness and while doing so he's molding us into his image that's sanctification and then he gives us away to the masses that's ministry.

It was thru seeing my mother's sacrificial love for me and my sister and getting a revelation of the love of God that I realized that real love entails sacrifice. There will never be a sacrifice made that brought, so many sons and daughters into the family of God such as the death, burial, and resurrection of Jesus Christ. I'm thankful for God allowing me to experience love thru sacrifice demonstrated before me thru a loving mother that sacrificed in many ways to raise my sister and I. Some might say well that's what parents are supposed to do. I might answer hats off to every parent or guardian that has sacrificed to raise children and demonstrate the love of God. Although parents are supposed to provide for their children I dedicated this chapter to my mother and all those who have answered the call because there are many that did not. Blessings to you! It was thru the love my mother had for us which was demonstrated thru sacrifice that I learned when you really love someone you will be willing to make sacrifices to contribute to their wellbeing. It was thru her example that I received my work ethic. I realized anything worth having usually requires hard work and most of all I thank her so much for showing me how to put God first no matter what season I am in my life. Much love to you Momma.

A RECIPE FOR WALKING IN LOVE

"Be ye therefore followers of God, as dear children; And walk in love, as Christ also hath loved us, and hath given himself for us an offering and a sacrifice to God for a sweet-smelling savour" Ephesians 5:1-2(KJV). Ephesians 5:1-2 (NLT) says, *"Imitate God, therefore, in everything you do, because you are his dear children. Live a life filled with love, following the example of Christ. He loved us and offered himself as a sacrifice for us, a pleasing aroma to God."*

Love shown by inspiration was my Auntie Rose. My aunt is another angel that God placed in my life to teach me love. One of the things that I found out about love is that love is a sign that an individual has been touched by the hand of God. I'm not talking about love that's based upon performance meaning I only love you if you meet my list of requirements, but it is one of the Greek words for love, which is Agape. This word means benevolent; unselfish love. Some believe that a way to know if someone is saved is to look at their spiritual gifts, and activities, such as how many scriptures they can quote, can they preach or sing under the anointing, but Jesus said in John 13:35 (KJV) *"By this shall all men know that ye are my disciples, if ye have love one to another."*

My Auntie Rose was a lady that walked in so much love that the love of God that surrounded her was like a spiritual magnetic force that drew people in. It was so strong that sinners and saints just loved to be in her presence. She lived in the country in a white house with a front porch with a screen door. There were usually always people sitting on her porch and usually somebody walking in through that screen door. I was born in Liberty, Texas but grew up in Houston, so I didn't understand why she would let all those people in her house, but later I found out the answer. People were drawn to her and she didn't turn them away. She loved God, people, and in return many loved her. I believe Auntie Rose may have had a calling to counsel people.

People there were blessed because they got a lot of free counsel. She had this way of making you feel like you were the most important person in the world. The love in her made you realize that you are special in God's sight and hers. The love she showed you made you feel safe like you could bare your soul to her and not worry about her repeating your business. I could sense the love she had for me. When I walked in the room she would light up every time she saw me. I can honestly say she was the only one that could call me Bookie as a grown man. I never sensed a mixture coming from her like hate one moment and love the next. I always sensed love. She never said one cruel word to me. Don't get me wrong I know that they're no perfect people, but I do believe that as Christians that we are called to be salt and light (Matthew 5:13). We are called to impact this world with the love of God.

My Auntie Rose was born with Polio, so she wore leg braces, but she never let her condition keep her from serving God and loving people. She went on to be with the Lord. My Auntie was an awesome cook and loved to feed people. She knew one of my favorite things to eat was fried chicken, so whenever she knew I would be in town she fried chicken for me. I used to wonder why I loved to eat her cooking so much, I later realized that it wasn't just because she was an excellent cook, but also because the meal was prepared with love. Right before she passed, I can remember when she was sick and was cooking less. At this time no one really knew the nature of her illness. One particular day it seemed like her heart was set on cooking for me and I didn't want her to worry about cooking. I came over and she sat down in a chair in front of her hot stove and cooked probably one of her best meals she had cooked me. It was guess, fried chicken with macaroni and cheese, green beans, and cornbread. It looked like she put all of her heart in making that meal. We talked and enjoyed one another's company. I use to always joke with her by saying, "I don't want you to think I just love you for your chicken" and she would smile and laugh.

She passed a little while later probably less than a year. We later found that she had cancer, but nobody knew it. The day she passed I'm not ashamed to say I cried like a baby because in this world one can usually receive unconditional love from parents and family and if you have anyone else that shows you sincere unconditional love you're blessed. Please cherish and honor them. One of the things I miss about her was that I could call her at any time and she would talk to me. Nowadays we text, tweet, facebook, and email. These methods of communication can be tools to communicate with people all over the world, but let's not lose the privilege we have of visiting those we love and sometimes picking up the phone to tell others you love them. Let's not replace the human touch with social media. Savor the moments with loved ones. Hug them, tell them you love them, visit them, and enjoy listening to other voices on the phone and in person. Let's stop rushing through life passing up potential memories that we could make by slowing down and redeeming the time.

Love Challenge:
This is your homework assignment and love challenge. Call at least three people you love that you haven't talked to in a while and tell them you love them.

CHAPTER 4

A Recipe for Christ-like Leadership

Scriptural reference: I. Corinthians 11:1 (Amplified Version) says, *"PATTERN YOURSELVES after me [follow my example], as I imitate and follow Christ (the Messiah)."*

LEADERSHIP IS DEFINED AS:

1. The office or position of a leader
2. Capacity to lead
3. The act or instance of leading

INGREDIENTS FOUND IN THIS CHAPTER ON CHRIST-LIKE LEADERSHIP:

1. Connection
2. Compassion
3. Correction
4. Time
5. Patience
6. Love
7. Burden

Inspiration for this message is my spiritual father, Dr. Richard Heard, the Pastor of Christian Tabernacle Church in Houston, Texas. We know that there's no relationship on earth that can compare to that of our Heavenly Father, but I also believe that as God matures us as believers we learn the importance of being grateful for our birth parents, mother, father or those that took on responsibility of raising us and parenting us. When we understand the importance of godly leadership we learn to be grateful for spiritual parents as well.

As I write about leadership I was inspired by other Christian leaders, but I want to use this time to tell you about my spiritual father, Dr. Richard Heard, who has been a huge inspiration in my life. It took me a little while to learn that although I'm a Pastor I also need someone to pour into me, help hold me accountable, and help mold me into the leader God has ordained me to be.

I met my spiritual father around 2006. It was at a very pivotal moment in life. I was being led by God to start the church I now Pastor, but I had experienced some challenges as a young leader in ministry. As I began to pray God spoke to me and showed me I needed a spiritual father. God led me directly to Pastor Richard Heard. When I met him it was an immediate connection. The Lord continued to confirm that he would be my spiritual father. In the midst of the transition I was about to make in starting a church I met my spiritual father. My family and I quickly discerned so much compassion that he has for people who are in challenging places in life. We also felt that same compassion as we walked into the doors of Christian Tabernacle the church he leads. I was amazed at how many things that I needed to learn and am still learning to become an effective leader. Through his leadership there were times when he has showed me things from a different perspective. That's when I really learned what godly correction looks like. It's times I believe that an individual may need to be confronted in love because of things they have done, but one of the things I have learned is many times godly correction is helping an individual see a mistake and then showing them the correct way to do it. God has also used him to show me the importance of investing time in the development of those you lead. He is a man that has a pretty full schedule, but yet I have seen him spend time with his family, lead his church, and cover many other sons and daughters in ministry and still somehow has made time to be there for me when I have needed his guidance.

I can sense that he is a man with a lot of patience from the way he deals with people. It makes people feel comfortable to follow leadership when they feel the love of God in you. I have discerned and felt love in every conversation and encounter that I've had with him, although I realize we are grateful for godly leaders that God place in our life to help steer us in the right direction. There's no perfect leader, but when you connect with a man or woman after God's own heart who loves God and his people you are blessed. I sometimes get a slight glimpse of how full my spiritual father's schedule is and think about the fact that he's also a pastor, husband, a father, and a grandfather with so many responsibilities. I have also come to the conclusion that when God gives a leader a vision he also gives them a burden to see it fulfilled and a grace to help you fulfill it.

I pray that this brief message on Christ-like Leadership will inspire you to become who God has ordained you to be! I took a little time to talk to you about my inspiration to write "Christ-like Leadership" as I briefly showed the ways my spiritual father inspired me.

Now I will briefly talk about 7 principles to Christ-like Leadership. Remember there are many principles to learn on leadership, but I believe these 7 principles that I will mention will be a blessing to you.

CHRIST-LIKE LEADERSHIP

There are many leaders in our world, but Christ-like leadership is leadership which has its example from Christ himself, the Word of God, and godly leadership.

In I. Corinthians 11:1 Paul told the Corinthians to follow his example as he imitated and followed Christ. This scripture teaches me a couple of things on Christ-like leadership.

1. Christ-like leadership is leadership that lives in such a way that the leader's life serve as an example to their followers.
2. Christ-like leadership is leadership whose words, life, and actions are a reflection of Jesus Christ.

Paul said as I imitate and follow Christ the Messiah. Paul couldn't reflect the ways of Christ if he didn't have an intimate relationship with Christ himself. A leader's ability to lead their followers can only go as deep as that leader's personal relationship with God. It's something that cannot be mistaken for as charisma. A leader can have a ton of charisma, but if they don't love God and the people they lead sooner or later it will be evident.

I'm going to share 7 principles I believe are necessary to be a godly leader and lead those that God has ordained you to lead.

THE 1ST PRINCIPLE IS CONNECTION-

This happens when God connects the leader with the one they are to lead and both senses God has ordained them to be connected. It's a divine connection. Although the two meet in the physical realm it's a spiritual connection. It's what happened when Elijah, the prophet, came into the presence of Elisha who would be his protégé and successor in I. Kings 19:19. It's a connection that if handled correctly it can enhance the individual and enhance those that are connected to them and the kingdom of God.

THE 2ND PRINCIPLE IS COMPASSION-

The definition of compassion blessed me as I read it. Compassion is a sympathetic consciousness of others distress together with a desire to alleviate it.

Matthew 9:36 (KJV) says, *"But when he saw the multitudes, he was moved with compassion on them, because they fainted, and were scattered abroad, as sheep having no shepherd."*

Christ-like leadership sees people without direction, people that are hurting, and have a desire to bring healing, direction, love and the Gospel of Jesus Christ wrapped up in compassion. If an individual doesn't have compassion for people they can mislead and hurt a lot of people.

THE 3RD PRINCIPLE IS CORRECTION-

We live in an hour now that many snarl if it looks like someone is going to correct them. I believe that can stem from many things like many Christians have seen such misuse of authority, but it can also stem from one not knowing that when done in love godly correction is actually showing someone how to do something correctly which can lead to growth and maturity. I believe the Word of God itself brings correction to our lives, but in order to be an effective leader, a leader have to be willing to tell individuals they lead in love when they are out of the will of God or approaching a matter the wrong way. Jesus corrected the disciples in love. Godly correction is not becoming Mr. or Ms. Rebuke. I don't believe any of us that lead really love confronting or correcting people, but there are times when we discern that it is necessary by the Holy Spirit. It's not confronting everything an individual does or going around trying to put everyone in their place. It's loving them enough to speak the truth in love, teach them principles from the word of God, and lovingly teach and demonstrate the proper way of doing things. Only those that are wise will appreciate godly correction. A principle we can get out of Proverbs 9:8 is that godly correction leads to growth and maturity if it's received right.

THE 4TH PRINCIPLE IS TIME-

When you study the life of Jesus, you see that he spent time developing the disciples. He didn't just call them and lead them to fend for themselves, but he connected with them, taught them, equipped them, and released them to turn the world upside down. Any true leader must be willing to spend time with those he or she is called to lead. The disciples like all of us had issues and in most eyes probably didn't look qualified to be disciples of Jesus Christ, but spending time with Christ proved to be transformational for them. We see this in Peter who in Matthew 26:70 denied Christ, but was forgiven, redeemed, and restored in such a way that this same Peter preached under such an anointing that about three thousand souls were added to the kingdom of God. It's only by investing time with those we lead that we are able to see transformation.

THE 5TH PRINCIPLE IS PATIENCE-

Webster dictionary defines patience as bearing pains or trials calmly or without complaint. I believe we can also say patience is waiting and undergoing trials with the right attitude. In order to be a godly leader you must be patient with those you lead. Patience is definitely required when leading people because as people we are imperfect. If we are going to see growth in the people we lead we have to be patient with them. The amazing thing about patience is that as Christians we are shown a lot of mercy and patience from God, but we don't always demonstrate that to others when they make mistakes. I can recall feeling hypocritical when God showed this principle in my own life. I had someone who had been doing something evil towards me for a long time. I tried to confront them in love, but they wouldn't take responsibility for what they were doing. Then I remembered asking God why He was allowing them to get by with what they were doing for so long and before I could finish the Holy Spirit reminded me of a time in my life when I partied and walked in disobedience while knowing I was doing wrong. The thought came to me God covered me when I was in rebellion, but yet I thought he should deal with my enemies Old Testament style and quickly put some act right on them. Then a scripture came to me. In II. Peter 3:9 (KJV), *"The Lord is not slack concerning his promise, as some men count slackness; but is longsuffering to us-ward, not willing that any should perish, but that all should come to repentance."*

You see God was patient and merciful with me when I was in my rebellion stage because he not only saw my rebellion at the time, but he saw my future obedience that I would repent and chase after him with all my heart. When we lead people we must display patience not only looking at where they are, but through seeking God we have to be able to discern their God given potential and help them walk into the destiny that God has for them.

THE 6TH PRINCIPLE IS LOVE-
Christ-like leadership is leadership that consistently demonstrates the love of God. Imagine the amount of love the disciples felt as they actually spent time in the presence of the master. You could sense the love they had for Christ

and he had for them. John 21:20 (KJV) reads, *"Then Peter, turning about, seeth the disciple whom Jesus loved following; which also leaned on his breast at the supper, and said, Lord, which is he that betrayed thee?"* Now remember John is the author of this Gospel according to him. John describes the scene in which he, a grown man, leaned on Jesus breast at supper while calling himself the disciple whom Jesus loved. This displays to me 1. John felt really comfortable around Jesus and had the greatest love any man or woman could demonstrate when he died for our sins. John 15:13 (KJV) says, *"Greater love hath no man than this, that a man lay down his life for his friends."* II. Corinthians 5:21 (KJV) reads, *"For he hath made him to be sin for us, who knew no sin; that we might be made the righteousness of God in him."* Christ impacted those who followed him with His words, His miracles, His obedience to the Father, but also His love.

We live in an hour where many have experienced some of the most difficult trials in their lives. The love that mankind should have for one another is waxing cold even in some Christian circles. Many are persecuted and tried in the world. I believe the one thing that will cause followers to connect to the spiritual leadership God had ordained them to connect with is when they see and sense the love of God in godly men and women. In this hour the discerning spirit will be able to look past how gifted and eloquent individuals are and look at the fruit in their life and truly discern if they love God and his people. It is difficult for people to open their heart to receive from you and follow your leadership until people genuinely sense that you love them and have their best interest at hand. Concerning marriage, Ephesians 5:22 (KJV) says, *"Wives, submit yourselves unto your own husbands, as unto the Lord."* "Husbands, love your wives, even as Christ also loved the church, and gave himself for it" (v.25). So there's submission to God, one another, and love is required. I believe that there's a principle that we can pull from how we relate to each other in the kingdom of God. When a follower can sense that their leader is submitted to God and loves them they probably won't have a problem following their leader's direction because they have demonstrated their love and Christ-like leadership.

THE 7ᵀᴴ PRINCIPLE IS A BURDEN-

Burden can be defined as something that is carried; a load; a duty or responsibility; something oppressive or worrisome.

I believe that when God gives a leader a responsibility to lead his people he gives them a burden for the people he leads. A leader without a burden is a leader with no sense of responsibility. A leader with a burden is a leader who senses a great deal of responsibility to God and the people God has assigned to him or her. Habakkuk 1:1 (KJV) says, *"The burden which Habakkuk the prophet did see."* Habakkuk, the prophet, was deeply troubled by the injustice that was in the land. He couldn't understand why there was evil in the land and why a just God would allow evil to exist. Habakkuk brought his complaint to the Lord. The Lord responded in Habakkuk chapter 2:1 (KJV) by telling him to, *"Write the vision, and make it plain upon tables, that he may run that readeth it."* Habakkuk now had a burden for his people. He saw and was troubled by the problems. The Lord gave him a burden and vision of his will. Christ-like leadership will see people God ordained them to lead, get a glimpse of their issues, receive a burden to lead them, and a vision from God of what they can and will be if they follow the direction of God. Therefore godly leadership can see people right in the middle of their messiest hour, but discern by the spirit that there is greatness in that person and give them divine instructions that will lead them to the fulfillment of their destiny. It's amazing how God can burden leadership to help people see greatness that sometimes they don't quite believe themselves yet. When a leader has a burden for people it's a divine dissatisfaction that will rest upon them until the people they lead are walking in their destinies. By leaders having a burden for the people, God will give them grace to lead even when going thru their most difficult times while trying to lead God's people. The truth of the matter is leadership can be rewarding, but a challenging task because whenever you lead people you deal with different personalities and problems.

Habakkuk name means the embracer or the wrestler. Wow, he wrestled with the condition of the world, but vision caused him to see past his current condition and see a future manifestation of the vision of God for his people. There will be times when as a leader you wrestle with injustice, ungodliness, but vision causes you to embrace God's vision and lead His people in spite of the things that are thrown at you to derail, discourage, and destroy you. The good news is whenever God gives you an assignment and a burden to lead his people there's a preordained grace for you to get the job done.

CHAPTER 5

(Prayer) A Recipe to Becoming a Praying Man or Woman of God

INGREDIENTS FOUND IN THIS CHAPTER:

1. 3 Ladies God used to influence me to become a man of prayer
2. The Results of Prayer
3. The Power of Consistency in Prayer
4. The Impact of Prayer

One could use many definitions for prayer, but to keep from making the term prayer sound complicated I will use the Macmillan Dictionary. To pray means to enter spiritual communion with God for purposes of adoration, contrition, petition, or thanksgiving. Prayer is simply talking to God, communicating with him, and of course ending it in Jesus name. I believe sometimes people are intimidated to pray because they believe only the spiritual elect can as in only certain people such as, ministers, leaders, and deacons. Until this mindset changes we can miss out on the awesome connection with God that he desires for us to have with Him. As children of God we are actually all spiritual elect (chosen). I like to say that I personally believe prayer can be caught and taught. When I say caught I mean you can actually learn to pray by being in the presence of people that pray. Many of us learned the power of prayer initially through hearing some of our parents, grandparents, other relatives, and even church members. I believe there is an anointing that is released when you are in the presence of praying people that can have a long lasting effect on your life. When I say prayer can be taught I actually mean we can learn how to pray by reading the word of God and studying to find out what the bible teaches us on the subject of prayer. Matthew 6 is a great place to start in the New Testament. You can also go back to the Old Testament because prayer has been a tool that followers of God have utilized since the beginning. In Matthew 6 the first part of verse 5 says, *"And when thou prayest…"* not if, which indicates that as followers of Christ prayer should be a part of our walk with God.

I want to focus on prayer from the perspective of prayer being caught. Prayerfully at another time in another book I can do a more in-depth teaching on some principles from the word of God on prayer, but I will talk about my walk and how God used three ladies with prayer lives to influence me to become a man of prayer.

CHAPTER 6
THE RESULTS OF PRAYER

MINISTER LAURA ALMORE (MOMMA)

The first lady that I can say that really impacted me with her prayer life was my mother. I'm getting ready to say something that I believe you will understand after I explain.

I hear some people say I heard my grandmother talking to God and heard my mother pray and that's powerful, but in my case I don't specifically remember literally hearing her pray. However, I now know beyond a shadow of a doubt that she was and still is a praying mother. By me being raised in a single parent home my mother did her best to keep us in church and instill godly values in us. Going to church was a must when we were younger, but I had a season when I went through a disobedient phase. I knew right from wrong, but decided to do wrong around 16 or 17. I began to sneak and drink, smoked weed, partied, and got involved in other ungodly behavior. This went on even after I finished high school. I really believe that I was rebelling, but also trying to figure out my identity and how to become a man. I had to go through some things before I realized that I would not have peace until I turn back to God. I remember trying to get high enough or drunk enough to forget about my problems only to realize that after I sobered or woke up the problems and concerns were still there. The real peace I found out only came from God.

The reason I say I know my mother was and still is a praying woman because she told me how she worried and prayed for me. I now realize that she literally was praying a hedge around me and being used to help pray me back into a position where I was serving God. I remember one of the turning points in those days. I had been partying and I made it home late past curfew, but it was something different about this particular night that I couldn't explain. We partied, but I didn't have fun. We left the party to go to some ladies apartment. Normally I would be excited and the life of the party, but I remembered feeling sad and disgusted with myself. The conviction of the Holy Spirit was at work and I know my partners had to wonder what was going on because I thought I was a stone cold playa from the Himalayas and I acted uninterested in these young ladies. I just remembered feeling like the prodigal son in Luke 15. I felt like I was in a far country and I just wanted to go home. I made it home that night or should I say that morning. I remember thinking my mother was going to let me have it! She worked early shifts and it was time for her to go to work, but she surprised me. She walked out of her bedroom and her response shocked me. She didn't yell and she didn't scream, she simply said, "I'm glad you made it home." She then really turned up the God factor. My mom hugged me with so much compassion and said, "I've been praying for you, how are you doing?" It was the power of those prayers that prepared me for that moment. I broke down crying and started confessing the things that I had been trying to hide from and repented. I remembered saying I was tired of living this way. That day and another day I remember beginning the deliverance process. I was ready to go back to church and find out God's will for my life. Oh, if I could preach a sermon entitled, "The Power of a Praying Mama."

Some mother, father, guardian, or concerned loved one needed to hear this. God can use prayers to provide protection and release conviction of the Holy Spirit to help get the one you love on the right track. I know it's a time for rules, discipline, correction, and confrontation, but because my mother had been praying she sensed that night I didn't need scolding, but I needed the prayers she prayed and the love she gave that helped break the strongholds off my mind.

Love is a powerful weapon that dismantles satan's devices. The prayers prepared the soil of my heart for the words God would use my mother to speak that led to the harvest of a transformed life. This is an example of the results of prayer!

CHAPTER 7

"The Power of Consistency in Prayer"

MARY WILLIAMSON

The second lady I want to share with you is Mary Williamson. She is a woman of God who God used to teach me a lot of things thru and she also spoke a lot of things over my life. It was about the year 2000 when I met her, and I had accepted my call to ministry, had recently preached my first sermon, and committed to fulfill God's assignment for my life. I was about 25 years old at the time and recently made my mind up to serve God wholeheartedly. I felt the call of God and the anointing of God strongly. I also had this mindset that I wanted as much of God that an individual can have, and I wanted to be used mightily by God. I remember feeling like it was more to God and asking God for more. When you are hungry for God and the things of God you attract the presence of God. He fills those up who has a divine hunger for him. Matthew 5:6 (KJV) reads, *"Blessed are they which do hunger and thirst after righteousness: for they shall be filled."* While I'm seeking God I was invited to go to my prayer partner's house Evangelist Johnny Mosee. He told me his sister was in town and he wanted me to meet her. I went over his house and we all mingled and before I knew it we had a prayer meeting that felt like a prayer meeting out of the book of Acts. She prayed for me and the presence of God came upon me mightily. I began to speak with other tongues, so loudly as if I was screaming. I turned around and began to lay hands on people and pray for them. My life hasn't been the same since that day. Since then I have consistently desired more of God and have not stopped seeking God since then. After that prayer meeting Mrs. Mary began to teach me things about walking with God and she served as a spiritual mother to me. The greatest principle I learned from her was to seek God in prayer. The one word I will use to summarize what she taught me on prayer that transformed my life and turned me into a praying man is consistency. Paul taught this principle in I. Thessalonians 5:17 (KJV) which says, *"Pray without ceasing."* Notice how this verse is worded in a couple of other translations. New Living Translation says, *"Never stop praying."* The NIV says, *"Pray continually."* The Message translation says, *"Pray all the time."* This verse is not telling believers to do the impossible such as pray 24 hours a day every day. It's telling us to be consistent in our prayer life. This is also acknowledging our dependence on God. If you want to experience God's presence in your life in a tangible way on a consistent basis meet with him on a consistent basis. I remember Mrs. Mary making a simple, but life changing statement to me on prayer that has helped transform my life. She told me to meet with God at the same time every day. That's consistency right! She also told me I would have to stay before God.

I began to get up early every morning to spend time in prayer. After I pray I get into the word of God and I can honestly say after at least 13 years of consistently seeking God's face in prayer I am still in a place where I can't get enough of being in his presence. It really is addictive once you experience God's presence and realize the creator of the universe delights in His creation having fellowship with Him. I could tell you how many hours I pray or talk about praying all night, which are powerful experiences, but what I want you to get out of this writing on prayer is a desire to be consistent in prayer. Spend time with God every day. If you do these things your life will never be the same. When you find individuals that are praying people, you can discern that their life is stamped with the presence of God. It's something about prayer that releases a tangible anointing in your life.

If you don't pray continually every day I challenge you to set a time to meet with God every day at the same time if possible. I got to a place in my walk where I don't like to be late or miss that time with him. It has taught me to rely on him for everything and has me on a quest to know him (Philippians 3:10). I now understand what Paul meant in Acts 17:28 (KJV) when he wrote, *"For in him we live, and move, and have our being..."*

CHAPTER 8

The Impact of Prayer

DR. BARBARA GUTHRIE (MY MENTOR)

The third lady that I learned principles on prayer from is Dr. Barbara Guthrie who I consider a mentor. A lady who I have learned a lot from, she has covered me in prayer, and helped walked me through challenging seasons in my life. There will be times when believers will face spiritual battles.

The apostle Paul explains that we are to put on the whole armor of God in Ephesians 6. He starts off in verse 10 by saying, *"Finally, my brethren, be strong in the Lord, and in the power of his might."* One thing to remember when we face spiritual battles is to remember we are not standing in our own strength. We stand in the name that is above all names Jesus. For those who are saved we have the power of the Holy Spirit living inside of us which makes us more than conquers. In verse 11 Paul says to put on the whole armor of God. One thing that can be spotted by the enemy in the spirit realm is spiritually half dressed Christians. Believers who don't take time to learn our armor Ephesians 6:13-17 and put it on (apply it).

In Ephesians 6:22 Paul describes this satanic spiritual hierarchy that exists. It tells me that satan has an organized team of demonic forces that work for him and with him to help fulfill the devil's mission which is to steal, kill, and destroy. But what is so exciting and powerful is the fact that we have been given power over the enemy according to Luke 10:19. Satan tries to gain an upper hand by trying to prevent us from knowing our authority. As I walked thru seasons of spiritual battles the temptation was to begin to focus so much on the warfare that I would begin to magnify what the enemy was doing and minimize or not remind myself of what God was doing. God always had seasoned saints in my life to cover me in prayer, but while praying with me and for me they remind me that we are more than conquers Romans 8:37. Romans 8:31 (KJV) says, *"What shall we then say to these things? If God be for us, who can be against us?"*

I remember Dr. Barbara Guthrie saying a quote, "Prayer moves the hands that move the world." On many occasions I was reminded how powerful prayer is. When we pray the God of the universe is able to move on our behalf. Satan's hands are tied up. As we pray the plans of the enemy are bound, frustrated, dismantled, and angels are released on our behalf. We have the extreme privilege to apply the blood of Christ over our lives and those we love. It was many occasions that it felt like I was in an intense battle and Dr. Guthrie would remind me to go back in prayer and use the authority God has given me. Those seasons taught me the impact of prayer. God thru his word, his spirit, and his servants begin to mold me into a prayer warrior. I now go into prayer knowing things are going to shift when I pray, so because we pray knowing the impact prayer has, we pray with boldness. In the Amplified Bible James 5 and the latter part of verse 16 says, *"The earnest (heartfelt, continued) prayer of a righteous man makes tremendous power available [dynamic in its working]."* I thank God He taught me the mighty impact prayer has. You may be one prayer away from your breakthrough. Go into prayer knowing tremendous power is made available when you pray.

Dr. Guthrie also taught me to have strong intercessors around me. This has tremendously helped me in being prayerful about God blessing me with divine connections. I describe divine connections as God ordained relationships. I pray God bless you with divine connections that will enhance your life and help advance the kingdom of God. I challenge you to pray for divine connections. Many times when God gets ready to bless you he will divinely connect you with the right people. When satan tries to harm you he attempts to get you connected with the wrong people. I love to be around Christians that genuinely have a heart for God and love people. I pray God bless you with a group of believers that will cover you and your family in prayer. I believe it terrifies the enemy when we covenant with praying Christians we can pray for and have confidence they will pray for us. The bible tells us what happens when believers agree in prayer together. Matthew 18:19 (KJV) reads, *"Again I say unto you, That if two of you shall agree on earth as touching any thing that they shall ask, it shall be done for them of my Father which is in heaven."*

I encourage you to have strong intercessors around you. It is powerful when you are connected to other Christians that will help pray you through challenging seasons. The second chapter of Acts tells of how the Holy Spirit filled the believers on the day of Pentecost right after the saints were praying in an upper room. Many revivals have been birth out of hungry saints praying and worshipping God. Much of satan's assignments against God's people have been cancelled and dismantled by the prayers of God's people. Miracles have taken place and provision has been released.

Believe in your heart that when you pray that tremendous power is made available and things are shifting on your behalf. Commit to praying consistently, surround yourself with praying people, and believe God to see the impact of prayer.

CHAPTER 9
Thanksgiving for my Help Meet

Scriptural reference: Genesis 2:18, KJV *"And the Lord God said, It is not good that the man should be alone; I will make him an help meet for him."*

I decided to make this last chapter a chapter of "Thanksgiving." I felt I needed to take the time to express my thankfulness to God and to my wife for the ways she has helped me in life, inspired me, and continues to help me and so many others. My wife Cynthia Carter is a beautiful woman of God with a very gentle and beautiful soul. The help she gave me with this book literally reminded me of how we can get so accustomed to our love ones helping us in life that we don't take the time to properly thank them.

I WOULD LIKE TO USE THIS LAST CHAPTER TO ACCOMPLISH THREE THINGS:

1. Express my gratitude to God and Cynthia
2. Explain what it means to be a help meet in marriage.
3. Encourage everyone that reads this book to be more thankful to God for who He is, and all the things He has done for us that we have failed to thank him for.

It took me a little time and studying the word of God

for me to understand that when God instituted marriage that he had an awesome plan in mind. According to Genesis 1:28, He designed for Adam and Eve to be fruitful, multiply replenish the earth, subdue it, and take dominion. God also created us to praise and worship him while reflecting his image in all that we do in life. After God created Adam in Genesis 1:27, He said it wasn't good for man to be alone and he would make a help meet for him. After God made Eve, he brought them together and instituted the covenant of marriage. In Genesis 2:18 God used this term "help meet" that if we misunderstand the meaning we may miss the beauty of the term "help meet."

I was talking to a misinformed young man in the barber shop one day when I heard one of the most twisted worldly views of marriage in my life. As this young man and I began to talk he first begin to boast about how it was okay for him to be with multiple women in a relationship as long as he could provide for all of them financially. He then went on to say that to him they were all considered help meets. With my eyes bucked I asked, "What do you mean by help meet?" He said, "They are there to help cook my food, pay my bills, help me do whatever I need them to do." I tried to talk to him, but I sensed his mind was made up and it would take more teaching, more prayer, an open heart to receive the things of God, and to get through to him.

What was God trying to convey to us about marriage when he used the term "help meet" in Genesis 2:18 said, "... *It is not good that the man should be alone; I will make him an help meet for him?*" In the Message Bible it reads, *"God said, It's not good for the Man to be alone; I'll make him a helper, a companion."* Lastly, the Amplified Version says the following: *"Now the Lord God said, It is not good (sufficient, satisfactory)*

*that the man should be alone; I will make him a helper meet
(suitable, adapted, complimentary) for him."*

The word meet is not a degrading position for the woman.
The verb form basically means to aid or supply that which
the individual cannot provide. For himself the sep-tuagint
translates it boethlos, a word the New Testament uses in the
sense of "physician." It conveys the idea of aiding someone
in need such as the oppressed. Certainly a godly woman
meets this need of man. The word meet comes from the
Hebrew word meaning, "opposite." Literally it is according
to the opposite of him, meaning that she will complement
and correspond to him. She is to be equal to and adequate
for man. She is also made in the image of God. Thus, again
equal to man and not on the animal level being. (From
Nelson King James Study Bible)

I would like to thank God for my wife Cynthia Carter.
As I reflect back on when we first met, I realized just how
much Cynthia has spiritually matured and grown over the
years. I recall where we were when we first met. We were at
a night club called, "Oasis" in Houston, Texas. I wouldn't
advise anyone to go looking for a mate in the club, but this
is truly how we met. It was February 15, 1997 the day after
Valentine's Day. It was a cold night and I was tired of going
to the clubs, drinking, partying, and living a wild lifestyle. I
was saved at a young age, but like the son in Luke 15 I had a
far country phase in my life. I had spent years getting high,
partying and living a life that was contrary to the way I was
raised. The feeling I had this night was that I was ready for
a change.

I remember thinking that if God would bless me to meet
a special young lady that I would settle down and retire as
a playa (meaning stop seeing multiple women who I had no
plans on committing to). Normally when I went to a club

I usually had two partners with me. This night I felt like riding solo. As I get in the club it didn't take me long to notice Cynthia. It was like a scene from a love story. I saw her across a crowded room and I knew I had to get to know her. One thing I remember in my wild days was that I wasn't afraid of rejection. Cynthia's beauty caught my attention. I wanted to know her and wouldn't allow anything to get in my way. She had some guy (occupying space) trying to talk to her. I politely said excuse me and cut in between them and started talking to her. The guy got the picture and walked off and I started talking to her. I asked her for her phone number and did something that was against my guidelines in that day. I said I'm going to call you tonight. She said (yeah right). The rule back then was that when you meet someone you wait three days before you call them, so you wouldn't look desperate. When you connect with destiny you forget proper playa protocol. I still remember to this day the words that came out of my mouth. When she said, "yeah right." I said, "I'm serious, I want to make sure that nothing happens that could be detrimental to my future." We both went home and I called her probably about 2 or 3am in the morning and we talked till the break of dawn. I asked her if she wanted to go to church with me and she said she couldn't. Later she explained she was scared because she didn't know me. From the moment we met my life continued to change. I begin to change in a way that surprised everyone that knew me. Cynthia and I began to be friends and date. My partners at the time saw less of me and slowly watched me leave partying and drinking behind me. As I look back I realized, I wasn't rejecting them, but I was literally "growing up." I realized that it was time to begin to live for God and quit living life as if there was no tomorrow.

It was during the time that Cynthia and I was dating

that I sensed that God was calling me to preach the word. As I explained in an earlier chapter, God connected me with my late great Uncle Charlie and Pastor Delbert Mack who helped me understand what God was doing in my life. By this time I knew that I needed to obey God. I remember sharing with Cynthia that I was called to preach and how she reacted. I thought it would be like an emotional scene from a movie, she would cry, and tell me how wonderful this was, but that wasn't her response. She looked surprised and said, "Are you sure?" I said, "Yes." I began to chase after God with all my heart. I later realized that I was expecting her to be excited and amazed without realizing that if we were going to stay together both of our lives were about to change tremendously. She showed me her support and God begin to work mightily in both of our lives. I preached my first sermon in the year 2000. We got married in 2002, I got ordained at the church I began attending and became Pastor of that congregation. Every time I made a move Cynthia was there to make the move with me. Cynthia was young, no experience of being a pastor's wife, but she said yes to the assignment and never turned back.

I experienced some challenges while pastoring at a young age, but God gave me wisdom, courage, and direction. Around 2005, I was led by God to resign from the position of pastoring the church I was at and started the ministry we now lead Temple of Deliverance Church. It was a difficult transition, but God covered me and Cynthia was with me every step of the way. I remember fasting and praying before making the decision, God kept confirming that it was the right thing to do. I recall sharing with Cynthia what God was leading me to do. Again I was expecting her to give me some deep emotional answer, but she didn't. She simply said, "You said you prayed about it and that's all I need to know." Later I realized she didn't say this to be insensitive or passive, but she said it because she really believed in my relationship with God and felt confident that I would not make that kind of move without really seeking God's face in prayer. It still moves me to this day when I consider that my wife trusts in God and in me to be the spiritual leader of our home.

We started Temple of Deliverance Church in 2006 and my wife, Cynthia, has been there every step of the way. She has served in so many roles such as assistant, intercessor, teacher, or anything that needs to be done. I often have to go and get her out of the church because she is taking inventory on what supplies we need or cleaning the church. She does whatever needs to be done. I know some may be thinking, "Why don't they appoint someone else to do those things?" We have people, but my wife continues to serve in areas that she doesn't have to. God has blessed us to have my family serving with us in the ministry, her family, and many other precious saints.

I wanted to take this time to thank God for a wife that has been there with me every step of the way. Cynthia has put her whole heart in helping me carry out the vision God has given us. I recall how there were some sacrifices we had to make to start a ministry. Before God blessed us with a home I remember feeling discouraged one day and telling Cynthia I felt bad that I wasn't able to provide her with a home yet. She wrote me a letter and said, "It doesn't matter where we are as long as I'm with you." At that point I begin to understand what it means to have a "help meet." It's about being blessed to have someone who will walk with you in this journey called life and be willing to be with you thru the storm and rain, in the valleys or on the mountain top. When God blesses a man or woman of God with a husband or wife he has a mission for that couple. Their submission (coming under a mission) to God's assignment will determine the level of joy, peace, and rewards they experience as a couple. Cynthia said yes to God and has evolved into a beautiful and powerful woman of God.

THANKSGIVING TO GOD

I thank you God for being my Father. I thank you for saving me and showing me your destiny for my life. I thank you for leading me every step of the way. I thank you that your grace and mercy trumps all my failures, sins, and short comings. I thank you for my family and all the people you have divinely connected me with to help fulfill my assignment in life. I thank you for Cynthia who has been a help meet indeed.

THANKSGIVING TO CYNTHIA

Cynthia I want to thank you for the love you show me unconditionally. Thank you for brightening my day with your smile. Thank you for believing in me. Thank you for saying yes to my proposal, and saying yes to God. Thank you for the sacrifice you have made to help me fulfill God's purpose and vision for our lives. Thank you for simply being you. I love and appreciate you.

CHAPTER 10
Closing

BLESSINGS UPON YOU

In my introduction I asked you, "Are you at a place in your life where you no longer want to waste any more precious time and desire to see kingdom results?"

My purpose in writing this book is not to say the lessons shared will solve every problem in your life. However it is to inspire you and remind you when we are:

- Connected to the right source which is Jesus Christ.
- Have the right ingredient which is a craving for wisdom.
- Have an open heart to receive the right instructions from the word of God and godly counsel.

If we follow these instructions then we can experience blessings and kingdom results consistently in spite of any adversity we may face. Seek God with all of your heart and ask God to connect you with godly people, study the Word of God, receive wise counsel, and watch God move mightily in your life.

SOUL FOOD RECIPES BY:

McKenzie E. Carter

CRUNCHY FRIED
CHICKEN WINGETTES

WHAT YOU WILL NEED

1 PKG OF CHICKEN WINGETTES
3-4 CUPS FLOUR
5 CUPS COOKING OIL
LOUISIANA HOT SAUCE
LEMON PEPPER SEASONING
MCCORMICK CAYENNE RED PEPPER AND BLACK
GARLIC SALT
MUSTARD
1 LARGE FRYING PAN OR POT
1 LARGE BOWL

INSTRUCTIONS

FIRST, TAKE WINGS OUT OF PACKAGE AND RINSE THOROUGHLY. IN A LARGE BOWL PLACE MUSTARD ON WINGS AND MAKE SURE YOU COVER BOTH SIDES EVENLY.

SECOND, PUT ENOUGH FLOUR IN BOWL TO THOROUGHLY COVER CHICKEN ON BOTH SIDES.

THIRD, POUR HOT SAUCE OVER WINGS. COVER WITH FOIL PAPER AND SHAKE IT REALLY WELL.

FOURTH, POUR COOKING OIL INTO PAN, TURN STOVE ON, AND LET BEGIN TO GET HOT. WHILE COOKING OIL IS GETTING HOT, SEASON WINGS. PUT MCCORMICK BLACK PEPPER AND GARLIC SALT ON ONE SIDE OF THE WINGS THEN TURN WINGS OVER AND PUT MCCORMICK RED PEPPER, AND LEMON PEPPER SEASONING ON THE OTHER SIDE. ONCE GREASE IS HOT, PUT CHICKEN IN PAN AND FRY ON BOTH SIDES.

LET COOK ABOUT 20-30 MINUTES ALL TOGETHER OR UNTIL BROWN ON BOTH SIDES.

(STICK A FORK OR SHARP KNIFE IN THE CHICKEN PERIODICALLY TO MAKE SURE THERE IS NO BLOOD, AND IT HAS COOKED WELL ON THE INSIDE. BE SURE TO DRAIN EXCESS COOKING OIL. PLACE PAPER TOWEL ON PLATE AND DRAIN CHICKEN ABOUT 10 MINS.)

BLESS YOUR FOOD AND ENJOY.

YOU CAN SERVE WITH MANY SIDE DISHES

FRENCH FRIES, MAC N CHEESE, DIRTY RICE, GREEN BEANS, POTATO SALAD, ETC.

TURKEY WINGS
AND GRAVY

WHAT YOU WILL NEED

3 LBS OF TURKEY WINGS *(CUT AT THE JOINT IF YOU GO TO THE MEAT MARKET OR JUST CUT UP IF YOU GO TO GROCERY STORE)*.
2 TBLS FLOUR
COOKING OIL
1 LARGE ROASTING PAN
1 LG SKILLET
MCCORMICK RED PEPPER AND MCCORMICK GROUND BLACK PEPPER
MORTON SEASON ALL SEASON SALT
BELL PEPPER
ONIONS

INSTRUCTIONS

FIRST, WASH THE TURKEY WINGS THOROUGHLY.

SECOND, SEASON AND PUT INTO A LARGE BOWL WITH FLOUR AND SHAKE UNTIL WINGS ARE FULLY COVERED.

THIRD, POUR COOKING OIL INTO SKILLET OR PAN, AND LET IT GET HOT. THEN PUT WINGS IN SKILLET AND FRY ON BOTH SIDES, JUST LONG ENOUGH TO GET BROWN.

FOURTH, TAKE WINGS OUT OF PAN AND PUT INTO LARGE ROASTING PAN, AND POUR ENOUGH WATER IN PAN TO COVER THE WINGS.

TAKE ABOUT 2 TBLS OF FLOUR AND SPRINKLE INTO PAN.

FIFTH, LET WINGS COOK IN OVEN, FOR ABOUT 1-1/2 OR 2 HOURS ON 350 DEGREES.

TURN THEM OVER ABOUT EVERY 1/2 HOUR CHECKING TO SEE IF THEY ARE TENDER. ONCE THEY ARE READY, THEY WILL HAVE MADE A DELICIOUS BROWN GRAVY.

SUGGESTED SIDE DISHES

THIS IS GREAT WITH RICE AND THE SIDES OF YOUR CHOICE.

SWEET POTATOES, MAC N CHEESE, GREEN BEANS, GREENS, BLACK EYED PEAS....YOU DECIDE!

BLESS YOUR FOOD AND ENJOY!!!

Received Recipe from my Aunte Rose

NEW YEARS DAY BLACK EYED PEAS

WHAT YOU WILL NEED

1 CUP OF BLACK EYED PEAS
1/8 CUP OF DICED GARLIC
1/2 CUP OF ONIONS
1/3 CUP OF BELL PEPPER
MORTON SEASON ALL SEASON SALT
MCCORMICK PURE GROUND BLACK PEPPER
MCCORMICK RED PEPPER
1/3 OF A SMALL PACKAGE OF SALT BACON or SMOKED TURKEY NECKS

INSTRUCTIONS

FIRST, PLACE ONE CUP OF BLACK EYED PEAS IN CROCK POT, (PREFERABLY) OR LARGE POT AND RINSE THOROUGHLY.

SECOND, POUR FOUR CUPS OF WATER IN POT.

THIRD ADD SEASONING.

SEASON TO YOUR HEALTHY DESIRED TASTE. ADD ONIONS, BELL PEPPER, GARLIC AND BRING TO A BOIL. PUT CROCK POT OR LARGE POT ON MEDIUM SETTING IF POSSIBLE.

FOURTH, ONCE BEANS BEGIN TO SOFTEN PUT IN SALT BACON OR SMOKED TURKEY NECKS FOR ADDED FLAVOR.

NOTE (*WHEN USING A CROCK POT, YOU MAY COOK ON MEDIUM OR LOW FOR HOURS. BUT WHEN COOKING ON A STOVE COOK ON MED, FOR ABOUT 45 MINUTES, OR UNTIL PEAS ARE SOFT OR HAVE COOKED DOWN. REMEMBER TO TASTE AND DECIDE IF IT NEEDS MORE SEASONING, WITHOUT OVERDOING IT. SEASON TO DESIRED HEALTHY TASTE. YOU USUALLY KNOW WHEN READY, ONCE THEY ARE SOFT, AND HAVE A GOOD TASTE TO THEM.*

SUGGESTED SIDE DISHES

COULD VARY:

RICE, SWEET POTATOES, CORN BREAD, ROAST, FRIED DISH, OX TAILS....MAN!!!! ECT....

BLESS YOUR FOOD AND ENJOY!!!

FAMILY REUNION
POTATO SALAD

FEEDS 4 PPL, FOR LARGER AMOUNT DOUBLE ALL INGREDIENTS

WHAT YOU WILL NEED

4 POTATOES
7 TBLS MIRACLE WHIP
4 TBLS OF MUSTARD
4 TBLS OF SWEET RELISH
3 TBLS OF SUGAR
3 EGGS
1 MED OR LARGE SIZED POT

INSTRUCTIONS

FIRST, PEEL POTATOES AND THEN CUT IN CUBES OR SQUARES.

SECOND, PLACE POTATOES IN POT, COVER WITH WATER, AND BRING TO A BOIL ON MEDIUM OR HI-HEAT.

ALSO ADD EGGS IN POT TO BOIL UNTIL POTATOES ARE SOFT.

THIRD, REMOVE EGGS FROM WATER AND SET ASIDE. PEEL EGGS, AND CUT UP OR SLICE EGGS AS DESIRED, THEN DRAIN WATER OUT OF POT.

FOURTH, ADD ALL INGREDIENTS AND MIX.

REFRIGERATE IF YOU LIKE COLD.

GOES WELL WITH BARBECUE, CHICKEN, OR WHATEVER YOU DESIRE. PRAY AND ENJOY.

EASY LIKE 1-2-3
BANANA PUDDING

WHAT YOU WILL NEED
1 BOX OF VANILLA WAFERS
1 14OZ. CAN OF EAGLE BRAND MILK
4 3.5 OZ. OF VANILLA FLAVORED PUDDING
4 BANANAS
1 LARGE BOWL
OR 1 LONG COOKING PAN

INSTRUCTIONS
FIRST, TAKE PUDDING OUT OF PACKAGE AND POUR INTO A BOWL. MIX IN CAN OF EAGLE MILK, AND STIR.

SECOND, CUT UP 4 BANANAS INTO SLICES.

THIRD, OPEN BOX OF VANILLA WAFERS AND PLACE ENOUGH WAFERS IN THE LARGE PAN, IN 1 LAYER TO COVER THE BOTTOM OF PAN.

FOURTH, PUT BANANNA SLICES ON TOP OF WAFERS. POUR YOUR PUDDING ON TOP OF THE BANANAS.

LASTLY, REPEAT SAME STEPS WITH BANANA PUDDING, AND WAFERS ALL OVER AGAIN TO MAKE A SECOND LAYER.

REFRIGERATE IF YOU DESIRE COLD OR JUST BLESS AND DIG IN...

QUICK AND TASTY MEATLOAF

WHAT YOU WILL NEED

1 EGG
1 PKG OF GROUND BEEF AT LEAST 1LB OR MORE
1/2 OF ONION CHOPPED
1/8 CUP OF GARLIC
1/3 OF BELL PEPPER
1/2 CUP OF CHICKEN FLAVORED STOVE TOP STUFFING
MORTONS SEASON SALT
MCC BLACK PEPPER
MCC GROUND RED PEPPER
1 LG TOPPERWARE BOWL
1 BOTTLE OF KETCHUP
1 LARGE FRYING PAN
FOIL PAPER

INSTRUCTIONS

FIRST, TAKE THE BEEF OUT OF ITS PACKAGE AND PUT IN LARGE BOWL. THEN SEASON TO YOUR DISCRETION WITH MORTONS SEASON ALL SEASON SALT, MCCORMICK PURE GROUND BLACK PEPPER, AND MCCORMICK RED PEPPER.

SECOND, ADD ALL OTHER INGREDIENTS: *ONIONS, GARLIC, BELL PEPPER, EGG, ½ CUP STUFFING*, AND MIX ALL TOGETHER.

THIRD, SHAPE INTO A ROUND LOAF. PUT IN THE LARGE PAN AND COVER TOP OF PAN WITH FOIL PAPPER.

FOURTH, SET OVEN TO 350°. PLACE THE PAN IN OVEN. COOK MEATLOAF FOR ABOUT 50 MINUTES. ONCE MEAT LOAF HAS COOKED FOR ABOUT 40 MINUTES, TAKE OUT OF OVEN POUR KETCHUP ON

MEATLOAF SPREAD EVENLY, AND THEN STICK BACK IN OVEN FOR THE REMAINING 10 MINUTES.

ONCE FINISHED TAKE OUT OF OVEN CUT AND GET YOUR MEATLOAF ON!

SUGGESTED SIDE DISHES

RICE, MAC-N-CHEESE, GREENS, GREEN BEANS, BLACK EYED PEAS, CORN BREAD, YAMS, CORN, MY MY MY....ETC....

BLESS YOUR FOOD AND ENJOY!!!

CHICKEN, SAUSAGE, AND OKRA GUMBO

WHAT YOU WILL NEED

1 WHOLE CHICKEN CUT UP/CHICKEN PARTS
1 PKG OF OKRA 16 OZ BAG / USE 1/2 BAG WHICH IS 8 OZ
2 CANS OF TOMATO SAUCE
1 14OZ PKG OF YOUR FAVORITE SAUSAGE CUT UP
2 CANS OF HOT ROTEL DICED TOMATOES WITH GREEN CHILES
1 STICK OF BUTTER
2 HUGE POTS
1/8 CUP OF GARLIC DICED
1/2 CUP OF ONIONS DICED
1/3 CUP OF BELL PEPPER DICED
2 TBLS. OF SUGAR
MCCORMICK GROUND CAYENE RED PEPPER
MORTON SEASON ALL SEASON SALT
MCCORMICK BLACK PEPPER
GREASE
2 TBLS. OF VINEGAR
2 CANS OF TOMATO SAUCE

INSTRUCTIONS

FIRST, RINSE WHOLE CHICKEN THOROUGLY AND THEN SEASON WITH BLACK PEPPER SEASON ALL AND RED PEPPER.

SECOND, POUR YOUR GREASE IN LARGE POT. TURN STOVE ON AT LEAST MEDIUM UNTIL GREASE GETS HOT.

THIRD, PUT CHICKEN IN GREASE AND FRY ON BOTH SIDES, UNTIL IT GETS BROWN.

FOURTH, PUT BROWNED CHICKEN INTO ANOTHER LARGE POT.

FIFTH, PUT STICK OF BUTTER IN LARGE SKILLET OR PAN AND MELT. ONCE BUTTER IS MELTED PUT ONIONS, BELL PEPPERS, GARLIC, IN PAN AND SAUTEE THEM. ONCE SAUTEED OR BECOME SOFT PUT OKRA IN PAN, AND THEN PUT TWO TBLSPOONS OF VINEGAR IN PAN TO PREVENT OKRA FROM BEING SO SLIMY. STIR AND COOK UNTIL OKRA IS SOFT OR ABOUT 10-15 MINUTES.

SIXTH, PUT TWO CANS OF ROTEL DICED TOMATO, TWO CANS OF TOMATO SAUCE, TWO CANS OF WATER IN LARGE POT WITH THE CHICKEN.

SEVENTH, ADD OKRA AND ALL OTHER INGREDIENTS AND BOIL FOR 1 HOUR. BEFORE HOUR IS UP, PUT SAUSAGE IN POT AND TASTE TO SEE IF MORE SEASONING IS NEEDED. *DINNER IS NOW READY TO BE SERVED!!!*

SUGGESTED SIDE DISHES

RICE AND/OR CORNBREAD

BLESS YOUR FOOD QUICKLY AND GO FOR YOURS...

DOWN HOME DIRTY RICE

WHAT YOU WILL NEED

1 POUND PACKAGE OF GROUND MEAT
1 CUP OF WHITE RICE COOKED
2-10 ¾ CANS OF CREAM OF MUSHROOM
1/3 OF A GREEN BELL PEPPER DICED
1/3 OF A WHITE ONION DICED
1 CLOVE OF GARLIC CHOPPED
1/3 CUP OF GREEN ONIONS CHOPPED
ABOUT 2 TBLS OF SLICED JALAPENO PEPPERS
BEEFY ONION SOUP MIX

INSTRUCTIONS

FIRST, COOK ONE CUP OF WHITE RICE.

SECOND, GET A LARGE FRYING PAN OUT, PLACE IT ON THE STOVE, AND TURN STOVE ON MEDIUM.

THIRD, PUT GROUND MEAT IN FRYING PAN, SEASON IT WITH BLACK PEPPER, RED PEPPER, AND MORTON SEASON ALL SALT.

YOU THEN PLACE JALAPENO PEPPERS, GARLIC, BELL PEPPERS, AND ONIONS IN SKILLET, AND COOK YOUR GROUND MEAT UNTIL IT GETS BROWN THEN DRAIN EXCESS COOKING OIL..

FOURTH, YOU ADD YOUR RICE, ¼ OF THE PACKAGE OF LIPTON'S BEEFY ONION SOUP MIX, AND TWO CANS OF CREAM OF MUSHROOM SOUP.

LASTLY, STIR THE DIRTY RICE UNTIL ALL THE INGREDIENTS ARE THROUGHLY BLENDED TOGETHER. TASTE IT TO SEE IF IT NEEDS MORE RED PEPPER OR ANY OTHER SEASONING.

LET IT SIMMER FOR A FEW MINUTES ON LOW. NOW YOU ARE READY TO SERVE IT.

BE BLESSED!

AUNT ROSE'S
STEAK & GRAVY

WHAT YOU WILL NEED

1 PACKAGE OF STEAK (PREFERABLY CHUCK 1LB-3LB)
½ ONION CHOPPED
1 CLOVE OF GARLIC CHOPPED
1 CUP OF COOKING OIL
McCORMICK PURE GROUND BLACK PEPPER
MORTON SEASON ALL SEASON SALT
2 EXTRA LARGE FRYING PANS
1 LARGE TOPPERWARE BOWL WITH LID OR LARGE ENOUGH TO COOK
THE STEAK

INSTRUCTIONS

FIRST, TAKE THE STEAK OUT OF PACKAGE AND RINSE THROUGHLY
AND THEN SEASON WITH SEASONED SALT, BLACK PEPPER, AND RED
PEPPER. (TO YOUR TASTE)

SECOND, POUR CUP OF FLOUR IN TOPPERWARE BOWL THEN PUT
STEAKS IN BOWL, CLOSE WITH LID, AND SHAKE UNTIL THE STEAK IS
COVERED WITH FLOUR.

THIRD, POUR 1 CUP OF COOKING OIL IN A LARGE FRYING PAN AND
TURN STOVE ON UNTIL IT GETS HOT. ONCE IT'S HOT PUT STEAK IN
COOKING OIL AND COOK ON BOTH SIDES UNTIL STEAKS ARE BROWN.

FOURTH, ONCE YOU HAVE BROWNED THE STEAKS TAKE THEM OUT
OF COOKING OIL. THEN PUT THEM IN THE OTHER EMPTY FRYING PAN,
OR A LARGE PAN WITH A LID. THEN POUR JUST ENOUGH WATER IN
THE PAN TO COVER THE STEAK, AND LET COOK FOR 1 HOUR IN THE
OVEN ON 350 DEGREES.

NOTE: AS THE STEAKS COOK IN THE WATER IT WILL MAKE ITS OWN DELICIOUS GRAVY.

LASTLY, TAKE STEAKS OUT OF THE OVEN AND SERVE.

SUGGESTED SIDE DISHES
RICE, CORN, BAKED BEANS, GREEN BEANS ECT.

BLESS YOURFOOD THEN "THROW DOWN"

RECEIVED RECIPE FROM MY AUNT ROSE

MEATLOVERS SPAGHETTI

WHAT YOU WILL NEED

1-12oz PACKAGE OF SKINNER SPAGHETTI (USE ONLY ABOUT 50% OF THE PACKAGE)

THE KEY IS TO HAVE MORE MEAT THAN SPAGHETTI

1-10oz BOTTLE OF NATURAL CHUNKY RAGU GARDEN COMBINATION SPAGHETTI SAUCE

1-10 1/2oz CAN OF DELMONTE TRADITIONAL SPAGHETTI SAUCE

1 PACKAGE OF GROUND BEEF AT LEAST 1 POUND

USE ½ OF 1—14oz PACKAGE OF ECKRICH BEEF SMOKED SAUSAGE

½ PACKAGE OF BEEF WEINERS CHOPPED

½ GREEN BELL PEPPER CHOPPED

2 TBLS OF SEASON ALL SALT

1 TBLS OF PURE GROUND BLACK PEPPER

1TBLS OF RED PEPPER

2 TBLS OF CHILI POWDER

2 TBLS OF SUGAR

1 LARGE POT

1-XL FRYING PAN

INSTRUCTIONS

FIRST, GET A LARGE POT AND FILL LESS THAN HALF WAY WITH WATER AND BREAK SPAGHETTI INTO WATER AND LET COOK ON HIGH UNTIL TENDER THEN DRAIN.

SECOND, GET AN EXTRA LARGE FRYING PAN AND PUT GROUND MEAT, WEINERS, SAUSAGE, BELL PEPPERS, ONION, GARLIC, AND ALL SEASONINGS IN PAN AND COOK ABOUT 30 MINUTES OR UNTIL BROWN AND THEN DRAIN EXCESS COOKING OIL.

THIRD, AFTER GROUND MEAT IS DONE OPEN RAGU SAUCE AND POUR ½ OF THE BOTTLE IN THE PAN WITH GROUND MEAT, AND OTHER INGREDIENTS. THEN OPEN DELMONTE SPAGHETTI SAUCE AND POUR HALF THE SAUCE IN THE BOTTLE AND MIX TOGETHER.

THE REMAINING RAGU PLACE IN REFRIGERATOR WITH LID TIGHTLY CLOSED AND USE THE NEXT TIME YOU COOK SPAGHETTI.

FOURTH, LET SPAGHETTI SIMMER ABOUT 5 MINUTES.

LASTLY, DRAIN SPAGHETTI AND POUR INTO POT WITH MEAT AND SAUCE AND STIR IT UP.

SUGGESTED SIDE DISHES

GREEN BEANS
SALAD
CORNBREAD OR ROLLS
"DISH YOUR FOOD, BLESS IT, AND GET YOUR HOLY CHEW ON!"

MOMMA'S PINTO BEANS

WHAT YOU WILL NEED

1 CUP OF PINTO BEANS
½ CUP OF DICED ONIONS
1/3 CUP OF DICED BELL PEPPER
MORTON SEASONED ALL SEASONED SALT
McCORMICK PURE GROUND BLACK PEPPER
McCORMICK RED PEPPER
1 TBLS OF CHILI PEPPER
1/3 SMALL PACK OF SALT BACON OR SMOKED HAMHOCK OR SMOKED
TURKEY NECKS
2-TBLS OF SYRUP
2-TBLS OF KETCHUP
½ POUND OF GROUND MEAT
½ OF A 14OZ PACKAGE OF YOUR FAVORITE SAUSAGES CUT UP

INSTRUCTIONS

FIRST, PLACE ONE CUP OF PINTO BEANS IN A CROCK POT (PERFERABLY)
OR A LARGE POT AND RINSE.

SECOND, POUR FOUR CUPS OF WATER IN A POT.

THIRD, ADD SEASONING. SEASON TO YOUR HEALTHY DESIRED TASTE.
ADD ONIONS, BELL PEPPERS, AND BRING TO A BOIL. IF COOKING ON
STOVE, COOK ON MEDIUM ABOUT 2 TO 1 ½ HOURS OR UNTIL BEANS
ARE SOFT.

FOURTH, ONCE BEANS BEGIN TO SOFTEN PUT IN SALT BACON,
SMOKED TURKEY NECKS, OR HAMMOCK FOR ADDED FLAVOR.

FIFTH, NOW THAT BEANS ARE SOFT GET A FRYING PAN OR SKILLET
AND BROWN GROUND MEAT AND SAUSAGE TOGETHER IN PAN. ONCE
GROUND MEAT IS BROWN DRAIN GREASE THEN ADD TO POT OF
BEANS. ONCE YOU HAVE ADDED SAUSAGE AND GROUND MEAT TO

BEANS AND THE BEANS ARE SOFT YOU CAN ALLOW THE BEANS TO SIMMER FOR A LITTLE WHILE.

LASTLY, TASTE YOUR BEANS IF THEY NEED ANYMORE SEASONING YOU CAN DO SO IF NOT YOU'RE READY TO EAT!

SUGGESTED SIDE DISHES

RICE
CORNBREAD
"DISH YOUR FOOD, BLESS IT, AND GET YOUR HOLY CHEW ON!"
RECEIVED RECIPE FROM MY MOTHER MINISTER LAURA ALMORE